DECREE A THING

CREATING YOUR WORLD WITH YOUR WORDS

NANCY JOY DOZIER

ISBN: 978-0-578-45351-4
Editors: P31 Publishing, LLC
For more information, please visit www.nancyjoydozier.com

Back Cover Photo by Alex D Rogers
Photo Edits by Harris Davey Jr. and Eric Dozier
All artwork was designed by Eric Dozier
Any people depicted in stock imagery are models, and such images are being used for illustrative purposes only. (Pexels.com)

Printed in the United States of America

DECREE A THING

CREATING YOUR WORLD WITH YOUR WORDS

NANCY JOY DOZIER

TABLE OF CONTENTS

ACKNOWLEDGMENTS

I am overwhelmed with gratitude to Yahweh for His faithfulness. I can't imagine my life without his abiding presence. Abba, thank you for never letting go of me.

Eric, my love, my husband, my miracle, I love you forever. You show me Jesus time and time again. Thank you for believing in me and pushing me to defy fear by stepping into dimensions of my purpose. I am eternally grateful that you cover me with strength and vision. I would follow you anywhere because your heart is my home.

To my Courtney Gabrielle, I love you. You remain one of the greatest gifts and assignments God has given me.

To my incredible parents, Apostles Herold and Rose Aubourg, I love and honor you. You have prayed and prophesied me into my current reality. Thank you for your investment and for living what you preach even when no one is looking. I can never express how you have impacted my life.

To my siblings, entire extended family, and family of choice, thank you for loving me and believing in me.

To my spiritual parents and pastors, Apostles Rob and Melissa Jones, words fail me. Your covering, love, intercession, and correction have sustained Eric and me. Your pouring into us has given language to our future. Thank you for always reminding us what God promised. I love and honor you.

Tamara Holloway, I am so thankful for your help with editing this book. Your careful eye and attention to detail are a tremendous gift. Thank you for everything you do to support the calling on my life. I love you.

Jasmine Womack and the P31 Publishing team, thank you for your guidance, expertise, excellence and genuine desire to see others flourish. Thank you for making my dream a reality.

CHAPTER 1

IN THE BEGINNING

DECREE A THING

The Word was at the beginning. It became flesh and dwelt among us in the person of Jesus Christ. It was, and still is necessary, the Word is most potent, most purposeful at the beginning. There is a spiritual law that harnesses the power of the beginning, the first. Most often, it's within the context of the tithe, the first ten percent of our earnings and harvest that we are to offer to God, and bring into the storehouse. Observing a Sabbath, a day of rest, on the first day of the week is also a form of tithing. As a worshipper, I've come to understand by revelation that there's even a "First Fruit of my Lips", that honors God. It's the outpouring of my heart, the love and adoration that overflow in response to knowing Abba. It's a passion, an awe, a gratitude that is reserved for Him and Him alone.

The beginning of a situation, an event or an idea, sets the course. It establishes a foundation. The beginning introduces whatever is of the most importance and is fundamental. According to John Chapter 1, *"the Word was at the beginning. The Word was with God and the Word was God."* God and the Word are synonymous!!! They are one; the same. Everything, seen and unseen was created by the Word. The Word gave form, purpose, function, identity, and order to what otherwise would have remained as chaos. It is the undeniable common denominator of all creation. There is no day nor is there night without it. There are no heavens and there is no earth without the Word. The Word is the divine fingerprint of God that testifies to His existence, His omnipotence, and eternal nature. It is what has kept the Sun shining and in rotation from the instant light was commanded to be, and decreed to shine. The Word has sustained the reproduction of the human race since God sovereignly adjudicated the making of man in His own image. Since His initial declaration, He has never had to repeat the commands He spoke. The Word has upheld all of creation since the beginning of time. It continues to create, as evidenced by the discovery of brand new stars and galaxies.

Beginnings are crucial. The study of sociology reveals that a man is not just an individual existing in a moment. He is the combined result of choices, decisions, experiences, education, nature, nurture and environment. A fifty-year-old man, who one day wakes up and decides to leave his family, is the result of a lifetime of moments, beliefs, behaviors and convictions. To single out that one day without considering his beginning, would be a gross oversight of what led him to that decision. If carefully examined, his beginning may reveal a pattern of abandonment, maybe from parents and caregivers, who themselves suffered a similar loss. His origin may reveal deep rooted beliefs of unworthiness and self-doubt about his ability to lead a family. Maybe it would be revealed that he lacks a proper example to pattern after. And as the saying goes, you can't give what you never received. What if loneliness and isolation were so imprinted in his soul as a child, that despite how much he may love his family, his nature demands disconnection and unaccountability? Discovering these original events that influenced his foundation or "beginning" gives validation to the man he has become at fifty years old.

The beginning tells a story, it gives perspective to present forms of reality. Two children born on the same day, to families that live across the street from each other can encounter life experiences that drastically alter their perspectives or outcomes. Child A grows up in a healthy, loving, consistent, affirming and disciplined environment. Child A is introduced to art and science and is encouraged to be well rounded. Child B, across the street, has a different reality. Child B is exposed to verbal abuse, drug addiction, and lacks a support system to help identify and encourage his gifts. There's no talk of bright futures and dreaming big dreams for this child. Due to drug addiction running rampant, the family falls apart. Without much additional details, you can naturally imagine how these lives will play out, just simply based on their beginning, their origin; their foundation. That's not to say that people cannot defy the odds stacked against them to better themselves and overcome the challenges their environment presented. But without the grace of God, the majority of people simply fall into the prison of reproducing the dysfunction that plagued their origin. In reading John chapter 1, it becomes quite evident that what happened in "the beginning" is of the utmost importance. This raises the question; why the beginning? Why not the middle or even the end? Is the middle less valuable and not as crucial as the beginning?

If God knows the end of a thing from the beginning, then wouldn't the end be as significant? I have personally gone through situations where I have needed the Word as desperately in the middle of my toughest battles, as I did in the onset. The middle is when you feel like your mind is unraveling. That's when you question if God even called you, if He hears you and does He even love you. The middle of a test and a trial is also when the heavens seem completely silent. Despite your sleepless nights and desperate cries it can seem as if the sky has turned to brass and there is nothing but deafening silence from Jehovah. Not even your "trusted wells" can provide fresh release in the middle. Your favorite worship songs or passages of scripture that have ministered to you in the past, seemingly lack in providing the same comfort. It would make natural sense for the Word to proceed at the darkest, toughest, loneliest part of struggle; the middle. A sure word declaring that you are exiting a season of despair and darkness, attack or warfare would be greatly celebrated. A welcomed declaration of victory, reassuring you that you survived, and that God is with you would be received with joy. A word for your exodus moments, shouting aloud that the enemy is defeated, and that your mind is intact from the fiery trial you've just endured. A word at the end is also befitting.

But because our God is who He is, His ways are not our ways nor are His thoughts our thoughts. He has exalted His word above all His names, so careful attention must be given to His word and its placement. Gen. 1:26-28 always makes my heart burn with wonder. It says *"Then God said, 'Let Us make man in our own image, according to our likeness; let them have dominion over the birds of the air, and over the cattle, over all the earth and over every creeping thing that creeps on the earth.' So God created man in His own image, in the image of God He created him; male and female He created them. Then God blessed them, and God said to them, 'Be fruitful and multiply; ...'"* This was the conception of man, in the heart and mind of God. He created man, and gave him companionship from the beginning, because there existed male and female. He also gave him an assignment to have dominion and He gave him purpose by blessing him with fruitfulness and multiplication. But as we continue reading through Genesis, we discover that this passage is simply God's decree and declaration of intent.

Yes, He created man, male and female, He created them. But He doesn't actually form man until Gen. 2:7 *"And the Lord God formed man out of the dust of the ground, and breathed into his nostrils the breath of life; and the man became a living being."* Consequently the instant God spoke, the created man existed. Now the dust and the breath that was needed to form man already existed and was already in great supply. In Genesis 1, God blessed man, which translates to "said something nice or spoke well of man".

The blessing, which is the decree was released before man ever took a single breath. Therefore by the time his eyes came open for the very first time, there existed a spoken blessing over his life. There existed a word that God had placed above all His own names. There existed the ability to have dominion and subdue the earth, the ability to rule and have relationship. The ability to create and imagine, to lead and strategize, to walk in the image and likeness of God were already present, in the beginning.

CHAPTER 2

THE ENTRANCE

DECREE A THING

Throughout my journey with God, I have often found that the life and writings of King David, The Sweet Psalmist Of Israel, are a prophetic key that unlocks revelation. Ps. 119, the longest chapter in the entire canon of scripture is one such writing. It is appropriately nestled directly behind the very middle of the entire Bible, which is Ps. 118. Believed to have been used by King David to teach his son Solomon, the alphabet, this Psalm instructs on the integrity of God's Word. The first letter of each line in Hebrew matches to the alphabet, establishing the intentionality and order of the Word of God. This entire chapter gives the reader just reason to trust in the infallibility, faithfulness, dependability and power of the Word of God. Verse 130 declares *"The entrance of your word brings light and gives understanding to the simple."* I have loved and quoted this scripture my whole life.

I understood that despite the degree of darkness around or within me, the word would dispel it with light. The word would unlock understanding of God, life, purpose and any other mystery including myself. These words have given me confidence that I can operate in supernatural understanding though I am indeed simple. But what Holy Spirit began to illuminate, is the placement of the Word. Where I had celebrated the revelation of what the Word brings, which is light, I had never focused on where the Word was located. I had never truly seen that the Word was at the entrance. Yes, the entrance; the gate, the door; the inception, the inauguration, the beginning. How had I missed this incredible, life altering truth?

As Holy Spirit started to download this revelation to me, I felt like I was given brand new lenses. The Eternal Word of God is perfect, there are no misplacements of words. A scripture that I had hidden in my heart for years, as seed, had started to be unfolded and unwrapped to reveal a most powerful paradigm. There is a reason why the Word was at the gate, at the entrance. The hidden manna here is that God sends the word before the storm ever comes. It stands guard at the gate, at the entrance, before the enemy comes in like a flood. Before all of hell erupts in your life, the Word must be in position. How can a non-existent standard be raised? It has to be present before it is raised. The Word is positioned at the entrance, at the beginning because it anchors our hearts, when a host encamps around us. It guarantees that we will see the goodness of the Lord in the land of the living, when we're literally crawling through the shadow of death. When the wicked come to eat up our flesh and an army rises against us, the Word declared at the entrance produces an *"in this will I be confident"* (Ps. 27:3) type of resolve. It breeds a *"though He slay me, yet will I trust Him"* (Job 13:15) type of faith.

The slightest amount of time spent in Kid's church or Sunday School, which is what it was called during my tenure, establishes certain foundational stories about the life of Jesus. His epic baptism by his trailblazing, camel hair wearing, fire and brimstone preaching cousin is one of those stories. It's a destiny moment that literally begins the unfolding of the new and better covenant. Jesus choosing to walk in obedience and setting an example of humility, is rewarded by His Father's voice. The faithful Sunday school teachers would vibrantly relay the moment when Jesus emerged from the river, catching his first breath above water. He stood completely ready to commence his earthly ministry, when all of a sudden the heavens opened. They detailed how the sun shined so brightly, landing on him as though it were a spotlight. As a dove descended from the open heaven, the people marveled as they all heard a voice from heaven saying *"This is my beloved Son, in whom I am well pleased."* (Matt. 3:17) Did they tremble with Holy fear? Did they immediately recognize that this wasn't John's voice, which they'd grown accustomed to hear crying out? Surely they recognized that they had witnessed a holy moment. They got to witness the Father of Creation, affirm His own begotten Son. They heard the intimacy of a Dad pouring into His Son.

Once the Sunday school class taught us about this defining moment in Jesus' life and purpose, naturally the battle that ensued was introduced next. The Scriptures reveal that Jesus was led into the wilderness to be tempted by the devil. After being publicly celebrated and commissioned, He was led away into the wilderness to be tempted. We can't just float past this. Holy Spirit led Jesus, the perfect, sinless and blameless Son of God into the wilderness to be tempted by the devil. Jesus did not experience the wilderness because He was in sin or had somehow incurred the Father's punishment. Satan didn't draw nor force Him into the wilderness. He was led there because it was part of His process as a son. It was necessary for His development that He confront every appetite and take dominion over it in private, so it wouldn't subdue Him in public. *"For as many as are led by the Spirit of God, they are the sons of God"* (Rom. 8:14). The scripture is very clear in that sonship is based on being led and not being filled by the Spirit of God. A major key that I must point out is that Satan is a servant to our process and purpose. Abba allowed him to be present to tempt Jesus, just as he was allowed to afflict Job, whose heart was upright before God. When you are surrendered and are being processed on your way to your purpose, Satan is an invited guest to your wilderness. He must be given permission by God, making him nothing more than a slave to your purpose.

So it is very clear that Jesus was driven into a wilderness. I also believe that it was customized for Him. It was tailored to process Him. For 40 days He prayed and fasted, nailing His own flesh to the cross, just so He could qualify to be crucified on a hill called Calvary. He understood that how He navigated his wilderness experience would determine if He could be trusted to carry the degree of glory needed, to fulfill purpose. So, if the natural progression of the Son of God's victorious completion of assignment included the wilderness, why would you and I be exempt? He never cursed the wilderness or even prayed to be brought out of it. Wow! Jesus so trusted Abba, and so trusted in the leading of the Spirit that He simply yielded to the process. He knew that the isolation would somehow work for His good. He understood that His authority over the enemy had to be established before He ever entered into His public ministry. By engaging in fasting as a form of tithing, harvest was inevitable.

The enemy only comes for the sake of the Word. He comes after the fact to contradict what heaven has already declared, with lies dressed up as circumstances, issues, warfare, mountains and struggles. The enemy wants us to partner with his demonic decrees rather than align with what has been written in our book, according to Ps. 139:16. What he forgets is that a primary function of the tithe, the first, the beginning is that it sanctifies and consecrates the rest and releases harvest. He forgets that the decree of heaven over our lives was released at the entrance. God himself effectively tithed into our lives and destiny by speaking His Word over us, which will not return void, at the beginning. Despite what our natural upbringing and environment may have dictated, in the spirit we are Child A. We are reborn into a brand new inheritance and full of light.

CHAPTER 3

MOTION SENSORED

DECREE A THING

Unlike my husband, I am not naturally drawn to technology. I feel about shoes and lip gloss how my husband feels about anything made by Apple, televisions, and gadgets. Go ahead and laugh, it's ok... I'm just being honest. He typically has to talk me into upgrading my phones or purchasing a smart home device. But when it's a gadget, the benefit for which I understand, I'm sold. Such was the case a few years back, when he surprised me with brand new night lights. These were not the typical night lights that you plug in... they were tiny and motion sensored. He attached them to the bottom of our night stands so whenever we would get up in the middle of the night, they came on automatically. The instant our feet would hit the floor, there was enough light to avoid stumbling and brighten the way to the bathroom. How genius an idea; a light that was created to anticipate your need for illumination. Ps. 119:105 states *"Your word is a lamp unto my feet, and a light unto my path."* In the sovereign wisdom of God, He not only placed the word at the entrance, but He helps us understand the dual function of it being a lamp as well as a light.

The lamp functions to illuminate what's right in front of us. It helps us take practical steps, while not falling on objects, bumping into obstacles or even tripping over our own feet. The lamp keeps us from stumbling over fear because it ensures a steady footing, with each step providing a sense of security. I don't know about you, but when it's pitch black and I can't see, the lack of vision incites fear in my heart. What I've discovered about the lamp, is that it is within the realm of our own responsibility. You and I are expected to light it and carry it, turn it on or activate it. As in the parable of the ten Virgins, the burden of preparation falls on us. We are to ensure that there's sufficient oil to light the lamp.

The light however, has a broader reach and keeps us moving even when we are surrounded by darkness. The light shines on our path, which speaks of our journey, our prophetic purpose and destination. The light, which is the word of God, leads us to safe harbor. It provides hope that if we just keep moving, we will arrive at our destination, a higher place, a greater place. It typically emanates from where we are going, pulling us from where we currently are. We can't produce or control the light but we can align ourselves with its brightness and move in its direction. The Light is virtually "the light at the end of the tunnel," pun absolutely intended. It's that glimmer of hope that has the power to override weariness and physical exhaustion. It will cause us to keep advancing and pressing our way out of dark places.

Few things are as dangerous to a human's wellbeing as darkness, prolonged darkness at that. In an article published in *The Science Explorer* on November 9, 2015, Kelly Tatera wrote, *"Humans need light and interaction to stay sane. Without light, we lose our sense of time, and without interaction, we become consumed with loneliness and boredom. With this sensory deprivation comes the strangest, most unimaginable psychological effects."* Scientists can prove that humans mentally unravel when forced to remain in darkness. There are also emotional and physical effects that are attributed to lack of exposure to the light. Human rights organizations even consider keeping war criminals in dark caves or blindfolded for extended periods of time as being inhumane. It is a torturous and barbaric practice. Plainly stated, we were not born to live in darkness. We are drawn to the light because we need it to survive, to function, to be balanced and mentally stable. I believe that going through seasons of severe obscurity, feeling isolated and trapped by our situations can have the same effects. A heart that is troubled and a soul that is overwhelmed might as well be in a dark cave because that is what hopelessness feels like.

Here's what I've learned from personal experience. Whenever I've allowed fear and trauma to incarcerate me, it has simulated a dark cave around me. I struggled with a severe fear of imperfection most of my life, which I attribute to being a PK (Preacher's Kid). The isolation I experienced, at times, though surrounded by people, lots of people, literally crippled me. Afraid to make the wrong move, wear the wrong clothes, be perceived as unholy, I was judged by people whose presence in my life lasted a Las Vegas minute. Slowly succumbing to darkness, I was forced into becoming a people pleaser, which deprived me of motion and advancement. I had become paralyzed by fear. It took years for me to get set free from people. Embracing the fact that I didn't need their permission was like coming out of an underground bunker. It was the Word of God, in my late teens that provided the lamp to guide my feet out of darkness. Discovering God's heart for me as an individual, His plans for my future, His desires for me to be authentic and free was the light at the end of the tunnel. The Word of prophecy and promise over me granted me a way of escape from my misery into my ministry.

See, God knows the plans He has for you and me, as prophesied by Jeremiah, because He declared them at the entrance. He authored your origin, and set the course of your purpose by prophesying over you in the beginning. Your gifts, your personality, your bend towards ingenuity, medicine, entrepreneurship, ministry, intercession, art, social justice, family, media or whatever it may be, are simply the result of the Word over your life. If you're like me and at any point in your life attempted to be something other than who God spoke you to be, let me guess, you failed miserably. I've tried shutting off the Prophetic and just being "normal". I failed royally. When I pretended to not hear God's voice and not see the things He would reveal to me, Holy Spirit would just wait for me to fall asleep and encounter me in my dreams. He is so persistent! I've pretended to just be normal and not be full of Holy Ghost and Fire, fearing I'd offend others somehow. You guessed it... I leaked! People have started crying, shaking, falling out and even manifesting demons all while I was "trying" to be normal. There is a word over my life released at the entrance that won't let me live a lie. Besides, being anything or anyone other than who God made you to be is completely exhausting.

What is the word that has been decreed over your life from the beginning? I guarantee that deep down in the recesses of your spirit lies a decree from heaven, that predates your first breath, on this side of eternity. Before the thief ever came to steal from you, kill and destroy you, there was a word at the beginning. As a matter of fact, every thief that has ever come to your life, did so knowing full well there was treasure to be had. Have you ever known a thief to show up to an empty house? It is the weight, the worth, the intention and impact of that word that has attracted the attacks. It is also that word that continues to prophesy your purpose even when your vision becomes so blurry that you can no longer see the promise. The instant you set your feet toward moving in obedience to what God has spoken over you, motion activated illumination comes on. That's correct, illumination is most useful when engaging in movement. Go back to the beginning, what did Abba decree over you? Let that be the lamp that guides your feet. What did He establish at the beginning, at the entrance, concerning your destiny? Let that be the light that draws you out of every dark cave Satan would place you in. Once you can determine what He spoke, you must simply speak it back to him, without wavering. That dear friend, is how you simultaneously activate the motion sensored lamp at your feet and the light unto your path.

CHAPTER 4

DECREE: SAY IT LOUD

DECREE A THING

From the foundation of the earth, the spoken or declared Word has been in operation. It has held the power to unlock brand new realities, to create what is seen from what is unseen and establish direction with compass-like precision. The book of Genesis chapter 1, verse 2 narrates how Holy Spirit brooded on the face of the deep, present yet inactive. Although He is one third of the Godhead, Holy Spirit could not build nor create without instruction. He was legally constrained to await the command of Abba, God the Father. We understand that there is no force more powerful than Holy Spirit. The Spirit that defied death, hell and the grave by raising Jesus Christ from the dead. He is the Spirit of grace and wisdom which existed before time. And as supernatural as He is, He cannot violate nor will He override our silence. It is not until Abba spoke that Holy Spirit transitioned from simply being present to becoming active. Imagine the continuation of nothingness that would be present still, had Yahweh not spoken. What if seas and land had never been measured and separated? If night and day had never been established by God's command, there would have been no sunsets, no sunrises, and no seasons. A world without trees, grass, flowers, mountains, valleys, waterfalls, stars, animals, marine life etc... you get the idea! How bleak and uninteresting things would have been if Holy Spirit was left to just hover over the water, and never released to use His power to create. In how many areas of your life is Holy Spirit just hovering, waiting for you to release a command? What would your words create in regards to your personal growth, your family, your career, and your endeavors?

Job 22:28 says, *"You will also decree a thing, and it will be established for you; so light will shine on your ways."* There's a very simple reason why this truth is fundamental to a life of declaration. The only thing in creation to not be spoken into existence was man. God decided that man would be made in His image and likeness. This required what other creations didn't have, which was His actual fingerprints. He formed man with His own hands, and then breathed into him the breath of life. When left behind, fingerprints are an identification marker used to determine who has been in a certain place. Fingerprints prove that the individual used their hand on an object. Because of the sheer brilliance of God, no two prints are alike. So He used His hands in creating you so there would be no confusion as to who touched you, and was present at the beginning. As though that wasn't enough,

Abba breathed into man making him a living soul. His breath gave life to what was previously just a shell, a form. It caused blood to flow, heart to beat, mind to imagine, bone and muscle to respond to the brain, and for history to be made. The most distinctive aspect of man receiving God's breath was the transferring of DNA. Man was already formed in the image of God, but it's when the breath was released into him that DNA was established. How amazing! Billions of people are on the planet Earth, but we can determine if two of them have any familial relation based on DNA. Abba, formed you and me with His hands, leaving his undeniable fingerprints behind, then He deposited His breath, His Spirit, His DNA into us so we would know who our Father is. Guess what? You are your Father's child. You look just like him, in every way.

The mystery of God is evident in that even in creating and commanding this world to be, there are things He didn't materialize. He left it up to man to discover how to create fire. Man had to discover gravity, probably through painful trial and error. Man had to discover aerodynamics, medical science, agriculture and so much more. What's imperative to understand is that the elements for all these advancements and discoveries have existed since creation. Ever since God spoke the world into existence, the potential to fly space ships and airplanes has existed. The elements for curing cancer have existed from the beginning. But, Abba so trusted in His own word that He rested, allowing man to journey on the process of discovering his full inheritance.

Part of our inheritance as the Children of God is that, like Him, we can create our world with our mouths. Rom. 10:8 states, *"The Word is near you, it is in your mouth..."* Something could not be any closer to you than actually being inside your mouth. But so long as the Word remains in your mouth and never breaks out from behind the prison bars provided by your teeth, nothing will be created. You must lift off every demonic gag order assigned to silence you. Enter into an intimate relationship with Holy Spirit, and you will find that He moves when you speak. He is the difference maker. His breath settles on your words to bring them to reality. Your Holy Spirit inspired declarations provide a mode of transportation for your miracles from the spirit realm into the natural realm. Prov. 10:11 says, *"The mouth of the righteous is a well of life..."* Righteousness speaks of being in "right standing" with God; in relationship. It is the understanding that whatever we receive is because of Jesus. He imputed His righteousness upon us so we could access an inheritance we didn't deserve. So we understand that the grace, favor, peace, power, resurrection life and authority we get to enjoy are simply borrowed. It's from that place of understanding that we can then release a well of life from our mouth.

We often assume that a person who is vocal in their unbelief, always spouting off negative confessions, needs to control their mouth. It may seem like every time they speak they somehow find ways to release death on everything and everyone. Raise your hand if you know someone like that! The truth is that their mouth is not the problem. Jesus said, *"A good man out of the good treasure of his heart brings forth good; and an evil man out of the evil treasure in his heart brings forth evil. For out of the abundance of the heart the mouth speaks"* (Luk. 6:45) Righteousness or goodness is established in the heart. This is where "good treasure" is hidden or stored away. Treasure is something that is sought out, dug out or discovered and then hidden away safely. Are we not commanded to hide the Word in our hearts? This is why we seek after God; we study to find those hidden treasures of revelatory truth in His word. Our mouth becomes a well of life when empowered by righteousness, or the good treasure that's in abundance (overflow) in our hearts.

There is a very simple yet fundamental truth to a life of declaration. Nothing happens in the kingdom without a decree; a word, which requires sound. A decree is defined as a command, a mandate, a proclamation. It is an official order by legal authority, judicial decision or order; a law. The Latin root word is *decretum*, of which the past participle is *decernere,* from which we get the English word *discern.* In decreeing there must be the ability to correctly discern the heart and mind of God concerning a matter, a nation, an individual or whatever it might be. When you decree, you are setting laws in place by commanding elements to come into alignment with the Word of God. When someone is sick, you discern that sickness is not God's perfect will for that individual. Based on His word, total healing and restoration is His will. So that is what you command. You mandate that sickness leaves, and that Healing manifests. You take legal authority over infirmity and make a judicial decision that sickness is an intruder. The spirit realm operates by laws. Even the devil has to adhere to laws set in place in the spirit. He must have legal right to afflict you, rob you and operate in your life.

If poverty and lack continue to be perpetuated in your life and family, you must discern what legal right the enemy has been granted. It's not enough to just want or wish that the poverty ceases. You have to engage the heavenly judicial system and plead your case. One way to argue your case is by decreeing the word of God over a matter. David said in Ps. 100:4, *"Enter into His gates with thanksgiving and into his courts with praise..."* You have access to the courtroom of heaven, but you must decide to enter there on your own accord. Any violation of God's will and word over your life, once identified, must be dealt with legally. The Bible refers to the devil as the Accuser of the Brethren, and to Jesus as our Advocate. This is legal terminology, which reveals that Heaven has a judicial system and is governed by laws, not unlike any Kingdom. Sometimes we give the devil legal right due to unbelief, disobedience, unrepented sins, generational curses and a myriad of other things. Other times, the devil just gets bold and takes it upon himself to trespass and be in violation of God's word (law) over your life. But when the thief is found (discerned), he must repay sevenfold everything he's taken. When you decree and declare the word of God, you are contending for your sevenfold. It's how you ensure that you are given your portion and your property. Otherwise, what is the benefit of finding the thief but not recovering your sevenfold?

The word accusation is defined as a charge or claim that someone has done something wrong or illegal. Scripture says in 1 Peter 5:8, *"Be sober-minded, be watchful. Your adversary the devil prowls around like a roaring lion, seeking someone to devour."* As a child I would imagine an actual lion searching and hunting for prey. But Satan isn't out here physically devouring people. I've come to the revelation that his prowling to and from is an intel gathering mission. I believe that as he's going around, he begins to watch us to gather evidence. When we sin against our mates, develop the wrong attitude toward a neighbor, are unforgiving to someone who's hurt us, or whatever the case might be, Satan is taking notes. He watches and listens as we make wrong declarations "I'm so broke"; "I am unlovable"; "I would die if he/she leaves me"; "I'll never be like my father. I hate him"; "I'm not technically cheating on my spouse, just blowing off steam". Also, he's not omnipresent so that explains the prowling and going back and forth searching for victims. He can't be at my house and yours at the same time, so he's got to keep moving. He accuses us and brings us up on charges based on our own words, which formulate our beliefs. Words spoken over us by our parents, siblings, teachers and leaders can be brought up as accusation against our purpose and our destiny. The majority of the time, these negative declarations become what we eventually start speaking about ourselves.

Unknowingly, you have been declaring lack and poverty over your life, passing it off as a common expression. So when you end up with some financial issues and go to God in prayer for breakthrough, guess who shows up! Satan shows up to accuse you and to justify the spirit of poverty and lack operating in your life, based on the intel he has gathered from your negative confession. Perhaps there's also poor stewardship of money, and maybe even a generational curse of poverty that he also presents in his accusation. Using his mouth as the weapon of choice, he declares everything he can against you to ensnare you to a life of poverty. But likewise, you must open your mouth as a weapon to counteract and cancel the curse of accusation. *"With the mouth, confession is made"* (Rom. 10:10), so you must go before God to repent. Repent for the wrong declarations, the wrong heart posture regarding money and stewardship, and if need be, the sins of your generations that brought on the curse of poverty. This is how you activate the power of the blood of Jesus to cancel the false testimony against you. Repentance silences Satan's accusations and releases you from guilt, shame and penalty.

Once the accuser is silenced, you then must align with the testimony of the Advocate. What is He saying about you? He presents evidence that proves He was nailed to a cross to eradicate the curse of poverty in your life. He rose from the dead with all power in His hand, making you a joint heir to His inheritance. You are seated with Him, in heavenly places, so that as He is right now, so are you. He is not broke, right now. He is not a beggar, right now. He is not lacking any good thing, right now. Whatever the Advocate testifies over your life is the prophecy that you speak back and declare. It is the testimony through which you triumph. Whatever the Advocate declares automatically makes every word out of Satan's mouth a lie. Every accusation against your health, your mind, your marriage, your children, your dreams and your destiny become false when you choose to declare God's Word.

Oba. 1:17 says, *"upon Mount Zion there will be deliver-ance, and there will be holiness. And the house of Jacob will possess their possessions."* Declaration is a major key to ob-taining deliverance. I love the picture that this verse cre-ates of deliverance being found on top of Mount Zion. It then reveals that the possession of our possessions, is the direct result of ascending.

In the natural, climbing a mountain and reaching its peak is no small feat. It takes determination and focus. It takes great strength and the ability to proceed when your body wants to quit and your mind begins declaring that you have too far to go, so just give up. Skilled climbers only take things necessary to preserve life as they climb. They have learned that it's completely inefficient to drag along inconsequential items. The other significant fact that experienced climbers keep in my mind is the scarcity of oxygen. The farther up they go into the atmosphere, the thinner oxygen becomes. This means that the climber ascends with the knowledge that the cost of being elevat-ed and reaching the pinnacle is minimized oxygen. The importance of every single breath takes on new meaning the higher they ascend. But for the joy of conquering the mountain, seeing a vast expanse, and experiencing a different reality they are willing to climb. What you don't typically see is climbers who ascend while carrying other people up the mountain on their backs. Why give already scarce oxygen to someone who won't labor to reach the peak on their own?

It's unwise to attempt climbing up the mountain of God, with fear, doubt, unbelief, anxiety, and past hurts in tow. They will rob you of oxygen. They will suffocate you by placing unnecessary weight on you. You can't decree life and be in agreement with a report of death and calamity at the same time. You can't say you believe that you are healed by the stripes of Jesus, then turn around and confess that your grandmother and mother died from the same disease, so it's only a matter of time for you. Do you see how that's like trying to climb up a mountain and sacrifice your oxygen by allowing dead weight to suffocate your deliverance? There's a possession that is awaiting you if only you can get to the top of the mountain. You're going to have to empty your hands, your heart, and your mind of every contradictory weight so you can be free to ascend in faith, to a higher height in Christ Jesus.

Until you use the power that is in your mouth to establish and enforce laws, you will not rise above your situation into the revelation found on God's mountain. The fact is there are things that belong to you. Satan wants to keep your possession out of your possession. Your covenant with Christ has made a rich inheritance available to you. It belongs to you. But you are charged with laying hold of it by declaring ownership. You are not helpless! You will not die. You will not go under. You will not self destruct. Come on child of God, open your mouth and decree the truth. Not only does the courtroom of heaven provide the opportunity to silence the accusation and cancel the curse, but it gives room for testimony to reverse the curse and unlock the inheritance, by way of your decree. I prophesy to you, court is now in session and God has ruled in your favor. Now open your mouth and decree a thing. Say it loud!

CHAPTER 5

TESTIMONY: THE POWER TO OVERCOME

DECREE A THING

Sometimes we forget what God initially spoke to us. His voice and instruction can get lost in the midst of us attempting to "do His work". We must remember the word spoken to us and over us. It's imperative to have solid people in our lives who can remind us of the promise, when our world gets too loud. People who know and love us well enough to have knowledge of God's decree over us, are vital to the manifestation of the Word over our lives. They speak the Word back to us, even when we're seemingly so far from walking it out. Often the landscape of our reality is bleak, but God sends people to point us back to the word He decreed from the beginning. It goes without saying that we all must use wisdom in sharing our dreams and promises from God, with just anybody. Everyone is not interested in helping us contend for our divine purpose. Truly, there are people who are under the grip of a spirit of jealousy, who will often times attach themselves to us, with evil intentions. But that's another book entirely!

Even Jesus needed someone to remind Him who He was and what He was called to do. The Son of God, in His humanity, needed the word over Him reaffirmed. He had obeyed the Father and faithfully endured the shame of being beaten and hung on the cross. Naked and broken, He watched as even His closest disciples denied ever knowing Him. The promised reward of His suffering and the joy set before him had all but faded, when the Father turned His head.

The agony He was experiencing in his body, carrying the sin of all humanity, was only made worse by being completely cut off from Abba. Knowing that His cries would go unanswered, as He was literally dying from a broken heart, must have been agonizing. In the midst of unimaginable pain, Jesus is reminded that He is Lord, by a criminal at that. The most unlikely person calls Him Lord, and asks to be remembered when He enters His Kingdom. This common criminal confirms who Jesus was by calling him Lord. He reminds Jesus that the entire purpose of Him hanging on that cross was to be the most lavish and most scandalous display of love, from the Father to humanity. He had come to reconcile man back to Abba and to be the bridge that restored the reality of paradise. The criminal's testimony was just the decree that the Savior of the world needed to hear in that moment of complete isolation, accused of sins He did not commit. Anytime we rehearse (testify) the word, the same power is released. What happens if you need to be reminded of your decree but there's no one around? I believe that Holy Spirit begins to arise within you to help you recall what God has said about you. That's one of his primary functions; to remind you what you have forgotten. If you are discouraged or feel lost, sometimes you'll have to testify to yourself. Begin to testify and remember his Word over your life. GO BACK TO THE BEGINNING!!!!! By so doing, you tap into that same release of power and promise. As you speak, faith will come by hearing. Good God Almighty!!!! In faith, you can testify your way out of any situation. By praying the Word in authority, you activate the power of the promises of God, causing them to be fulfilled in your life. The word is alive and active.

There are 5,467 promises in God's word to be exact. They are all yours, every single one. David declared in Ps. 139:17-18, *"How precious are your thoughts about me, O God. They cannot be numbered! I can't even count them; they outnumber the grains of sand! And when I wake up, you are still with me."* My heart is gripped every time I read or meditate on these verses. It's incredibly overwhelming to know that Abba, our Daddy, our Maker, our Defender, has us on his mind constantly. Our finite minds cannot contain the magnitude of His thoughts. His goodness is simply beautiful. In testifying and decreeing the promises of God, over our lives, we can do it from a place of complete trust. The best ideas or desires we could ever have for our lives pale in comparison to the thoughts Abba has for us. He watches over his Word to perform it but we must apply and appropriate the Word. Who in their right mind would forfeit any of the incredible promises that have been given to us by God!

What does appropriating the Word look like, you might ask. I've met so many people who became disappointed or disillusioned with God. They believed and prayed earnestly for something, even "standing on scripture" and yet there was no result from their prayer. The immediate deduction is to believe that God failed or the scripture didn't work. Through the years I've personally had to discover the process of engaging in due diligence as it pertains to the word. For instance, Isa. 1:19, is such an incredible promise. It says, *"If you are willing and obedient, you shall eat the good [fat] of the Land."* It clearly states a prerequisite to eating the good of the land. It lays the burden of responsibility on the believer to be willing and obedient. Willingness has to do with the attitude and heart posture, and obedience of course is the act. See, there were times in my life when I was neither willing nor obedient. Other times I was obedient but unwilling in my heart, eliminating myself as a candidate for experiencing the good of the land. So no matter how much I believed that scripture, quoted it and prayed it in faith, it produced no results. Does this mean that God is no longer inherently good and no longer delights in prospering his saints? Of course not. He still lavishes His love upon us in ways we can't fully understand and certainly don't deserve. He still makes the sun shine on the just and the unjust simply because He is good. But this is about unlocking promises and obtaining keys to our divine inheritance through Christ.

Humble yourself in the sight of the Lord, and He will lift you up! These words to a favorite song I learned in Sunday School come straight out of the Bible. Simple but so incredibly true. Only problem is that the song leaves out a few words. See, 1 Peter 5:6 actually says, *"Humble yourselves therefore under the mighty hand of God, that He may exalt you in due time."* The adding of just a few words completely changes the perception of this entire promise. There's an actual quid pro quo that is laid out here; a this for that scenario. That's generally how God's promises work. He presents us with an "if you" followed by a "then I". The frustration of claiming promises that don't pertain to you can be beyond exasperating. [If] You humble yourself under the mighty hand of God, [then] He will exalt you in due time. When you humble yourself, you can expect that after a length a time which is completely determined by Abba, you will be lifted up. We're not given a timeline for what "in due time" will look like, nor how long it will take. Looking at the scripture in its entirety, we understand that there is no exaltation or elevation without humility as the groundwork, the prerequisite. However, humility is developed over time. Part of what makes testimonies so powerful and personal is the process of getting to the promise. People don't just wake up elevated, or eating the good of the land. There was a journey they embarked on to position themselves to qualify for the blessing. So there is not a malfunction with the Word, ever. In no way am I advocating the non-biblical mentality of earning God's blessing. This is not an argument for working to please or impress God. How do you impress the God who rides on the clouds and has created every star? Sometimes we just haven't done our part to join with God, through relationship, trust and complete surrender, so we can inherit the promises.

One of the translations from the Hebrew word for Testimony, means "do it again." The Jewish people in the Bible days understood the power of testimony. They embraced the belief that every time the goodness of God was rehearsed and spoken of out loud, it was prophetically declaring that God would do it again. He would confuse their enemies again. He would cause His people to triumph again. He would deliver His servants from the fowler's snare again, and be their hiding place time and time again. Not only that, but as they would testify, they believed the same power responsible for the initial miracle was released the instant they remembered and celebrated the good deeds God had performed. If the same power that resurrected Jesus Christ from the dead, now lives in us, then surely testifying activates that power and sets it into motion, for God to do it again. Testimony boldly communicates to mountains that our hope is firmly anchored in the ability of our God to deliver us, again. It pronounces to sickness that we have witnessed its destruction before, and therefore can stand confident in God's promised healing. According to the book of Revelations, *"They overcame him (Satan) by the blood of the*

Lamb and by the word of their testimony..." (Rev. 12:11). Once again, this promised victory is placed in a legal setting. Testimony is given during court proceedings, which seeks to invoke the power of a tribunal in order to enforce a law. A ruling is made based on the evidence that is supported by the offered testimony. It is a requirement that the witness speaks the unadulterated truth, once he or she takes the oath and gets on the stand. Communicating the truth of God, which is His infallible word, over our lives is the power by which we can overcome. It is how we enforce the law, barring the enemy from all illegal activity. The testimony of Jesus is the spirit of prophecy. Jesus, our Advocate, testifies through His word, of the victory that He has won for us. He testifies of the purpose, plans and promises that He's assigned to our lives.

My husband and I have received quite an education on testimony. He endured a severe health crisis in April of 2012, which sent our lives spiraling and shook us to our core. We were, and continue to be to this day, tithers, servants in our community and local church, God loving and God fearing people. We were the "good people" that bad things should never happen to. Incurably human, but desperate to love and honor God and His word with everything we had within us. What was originally thought to be a severe heart trauma, was downgraded to a major panic attack, and subsequently assessed as a near fatal allergic reaction due to a medication that was administered to him. This resulted in irreparable gastro-intestinal damage, that triggered the onset of extreme weight loss in a matter of weeks due to lack of nutrient absorption. Doctors told us that there was possible severe damage to his ileocecal valve, which connects the small intestine to the large intestine. Over the course of the next 5 years, there would be talk of dialysis for failing organs, depression, and months at a time of being bedridden. There were countless ambulance rides to the Emergency Room and entire days scheduled around, at times 12 medications. Over the course of the next 5 years, there would be talk of dialysis for failing organs, months at a time of being bedridden, countless ambulance rides to the ER, entire days scheduled around, at times, 12 medications. There were visits to specialists all over our city and super tough conversations about a future we had dreamed of that may not happen. I would stay up through the night nursing him, monitoring his blood pressure, making sure he was breathing and soothing his pain as best I could. Leaving for work I would beg God to assign angels to watch over him. I spent 20 minutes of my break driving home to check on my husband. I would administer medicine, try to get him to eat or drink homemade juice, and then rush back to work. Leaving him unattended made me feel anxious. When I would go to the drug store or grocery store for a few minutes, if I heard or saw an ambulance as I got close to the house my heart would drop. I would step on the gas, and just start crying the name of Jesus, afraid that something had happened to my love. It took quite a while to break that anxiety and identify that trigger as a demonic tactic to handicap me with fear.

I watched my strong, funny, energetic, playful, musical, love of my life literally walk through the valley of the shadow of death. We were desperate for a miracle. Traditional medicine was no match for the demonic attack against his life. Day after day, I watched as my husband was slipping away. But I also watched God restore life and breath to him even when his body was trying to give up. To say we've seen miracles seems like an understatement. We've seen the grace, the mercy, the love, and the power of God revealed. So much happened during this time, some of which we may never tell because it still seems like a dream sometimes. Even in the dessert, God provided streams as we decreed provision and restoration.

Not once did we ever go without a meal, or without having everything we needed. We never missed a mortgage payment, and always paid for our vehicles and all our living expenses. Even with medical insurance God supernaturally provided for constant visits to specialists and for medications some of which cost over a hundred dollars monthly per script... He was on several at a time. Most people who know us didn't have a clue about the severity of what we were going through. People would see me preach or lead worship with a smile on my face, encouraging the congregation to believe God and be encouraged. They had no idea! Not a clue of the battle we were in for my husband's life. We were fighting for our future, our promises and our legacy.

I thank God for Holy Spirit because He gave us wisdom, in regards to not sharing what we were experiencing with everyone. It wasn't about being secretive as much as it was about protecting what I started calling our faith bubble. As well meaning as people are, they can also be so careless with their words, causing the faith in others to hemorrhage. Completely unaware, people will have you forfeiting every faith declaration you've made and the word you're standing on. By that time they are through telling you about Uncle Jim, that Uncle that just got sick out of nowhere. Your symptoms sound just like what happened to Uncle Jim. So to avoid being rude, you listen with attentiveness and concern. Finally, finding an opening to insert your comment you lovingly ask, "How is Uncle Jim doing these days?" With no regard for your faith or feelings they blurt out, "Oh, Uncle Jim died! yep! But we are praying for you." To avoid potentially going postal on such people, in wisdom we chose to be very discriminating of who we told. Some people can't control their doubt, unbelief and negativity.

It was hard enough fighting to maintain our faith stance and decree life without having to undo the results of other people's confessions. And then there are those who really don't want you to get well. Some people are on demonic assignment to suffocate your faith and disable you from birthing your miracle. Throughout this ordeal, I was decreeing the Word, but I also asked Holy Spirit to show me how to pray specifically. I asked Him to reveal any hindrances or evil plots against my husband. I would pray through the night and ask God for eyes to see and ears to hear. One of the most pivotal moments came one Sunday morning, after I had been praying like this for a while. I had been up all night with Eric, but felt I needed to be in church that morning. My sister-in-love rode with me as we were both serving and needed to arrive early. She brought up a certain individual who had connected to our church, but she sensed something was off with this person's motive. She'd had a disturbing dream about the person on Saturday night. In her dream she saw that the person was trying to hide their identity as to not be found out for wanting to bring harm to our church.

Once at the church, we began preparations for service which included sound check with the Worship team and band. While the music was going on full blast, and the singers were singing, my eyes were drawn to the very back of the sanctuary. The person in question was arranging chairs and laying bulletins on each seat. I knew this couldn't be a coincidence, after hearing the dream and considering the strong conviction I had to not stay with Eric that morning, but to be in church. All of a sudden, Holy Spirit opened my ears, and above all the music that was being played He allowed me to hear this person praying. First, I was stunned that despite the distance between us, I could hear them above everything else happening. Furthermore, I was shocked that not only could I hear them, but they were speaking in demonic tongues to attempt to curse our church and my husband. Whenever I would hear that clearly in the spirit, it was typically while praying for someone, right in front of me. Holy Spirit began to translate everything that was being said. I had never experienced this in my life up until that point. I immediately began to cancel and reverse every curse they spoke.

I've always been very sensitive to the spirit realm, from the time I was a child. I would have dreams that would come to pass, just as I had seen. Back when we had landlines and home phones, I would blurt out to my parents who was calling before they answered. When praying for people, I would see, hear or have what I call "an internal witness" (Rom. 8:16) of something they had done, said, felt, or experienced or even desired. There's no explanation for how this gift operated in my life, except for what the Bible calls prophecy. I had grown and developed in my prophetic gifting through the years. The older I became and the deeper my relationship with Holy Spirit also became, I stepped into other dimensions of the prophetic such as discerning of spirits, interpreting dreams as well as heavenly tongues. So in terms of having experienced the supernatural, I had quite a resume. But nothing could have prepared me for this moment.

For years I had become acquainted with God's voice through Holy Spirit inspired utterances, but I had never heard a demonic utterance. I knew by how my spirit responded that this individual's declarations were not of God. This was no different from the times I had a prophetic sense of what a person was thinking or had said or even what God was saying concerning them. Only this time my prophetic gifting was operating to expose the plot of the enemy. The fact that I had prayed and asked God to show me hidden things that could be coming against my husband and I, as well as my sister-in-love's dream were powerful confirmations.

I don't remember when I stopped singing my harmony part of the song we were running through but I began to pray in my heavenly tongue, in full battle mode. In that moment, I also began to decree the opposite of whatever I heard the witch speak. They spoke death, I decreed life. They spoke confusion, I decreed a sound mind according to the Word of God. They spoke calamity and premature death against my husband, I blood blocked that curse and decreed salvation and long life to satisfy my husband. This went only for a few minutes, until the individual looked right up at me. As I stood in authority and decreed the Word, the individual became aware that I could hear them. Because my God answers by fire, I knew that someone operating demonically would not be able to continue to do so in His presence. I stood in authority, asking God to release his consuming fire and watched as they dropped the bulletins and hurried out of the sanctuary. Now one can argue that there's no way this event happened and that perhaps I'm too mystical. But what I know is that the individual never returned to our church, and my husband's health took a dramatically positive turn just days after this incident.

The majority of the body of Christ wants to pretend that witchcraft isn't real, and that if it is real we can live under the radar so long as we don't pick a fight. So what do you do when those on demonic assignment pick a fight with you? You better know how to hear and obey the voice of Holy Spirit, and you certainly better know how to fight back in the spirit. I was so grateful that the Lord taught me the power of the proceeding word from His mouth. Had I not known how to open my mouth and release kingdom decrees and declarations, those curses would have landed. By His grace, Abba had me in a season of learning, studying, praying and declaring the word of God. My husband and I both would fill our hearts and atmospheres constantly with scripture. Daily we played recordings of the scriptures being read out loud, knowing that faith would come by hearing. We would even fall asleep muttering, and rehearsing the Word of God, in violent protest to contrary thoughts that would attempt to hijack our imaginations and our dreams.

This is why you simply cannot touch and agree with everyone, when it comes to certain things. Everybody is not for you and does not have your best interests at heart. Ask Holy Spirit to lead you. Thankfully for us, our Spiritual covering, immediate family and a few inner circle friends supported us in prayer. They shared in our faith and in our declaration. And when we were weak, their prayers and decrees carried us. And there were many, many, many days of weakness. There were many days of tears and wondering. There were way too many days spent in hospitals and doctors offices, even though our confession and decree was that of divine healing. There were nights neither of us slept all night because Eric was in tremendous pain. There were times I would awaken to my husband being unable to breathe, and had to literally command breath back into his body. There were times I turned the shower on and stood in there crying, asking God to help me focus on His promises and not our reality, as I felt my mind unraveling. Some days it seemed that the more we prayed, the worse it would get. We would be so encouraged by a prophetic word, a dream or just God's presence filling our home and the next day would once more be in the back of an ambulance.

After months of being too weak to play any of his instruments, Eric had mustered enough strength to compose for me a "goodbye song". Though probably one of the most beautiful songs I've ever heard in my life, I couldn't receive it. With tears streaming down my face, I explained that he was not allowed to give up and that saying "goodbye" was not something he and I would do for at least another 70 years. He just wasn't allowed to sing that song. The decree of healing doesn't negate your humanity, it simply must override it. The confession has to be so deeply rooted in your heart, that it becomes the automated response when fear comes. It took diligence to establish declaration as a non-negotiable discipline in our life, but am I ever so grateful we didn't give up. The proof is that God performed supernatural wonders in our life. There is so much that has happened that doctors still can't explain, such as how my husband to this day has never had a single dialysis treatment and NEVER will. They can't explain how that ileocecal valve somehow was made brand new. They don't know how all the holes are gone and full function has resumed. It doesn't make sense to the natural mind that my husband now travels around the world, doing what we were told he never would again; playing music. They can't explain how God cancelled my husband's funeral.

There are still days when challenges come and sickness tries to settle back in. But, we understand how to open our mouths and remind infirmity that it was nailed to the cross. We haven't arrived at some type of faith pinnacle. It took us years to get to where we are now and to learn these lessons about decreeing the Word of God. Our journey is a process and we are still being perfected. For the brave soul who embarks on a life of declaration, the words of Jesus must become the designated motto; "*Give us this day our daily bread.*" (Matt. 6:11) Like bread, the Word of God must be declared daily to feed faith. Daily decisions must be made to believe and speak the Word of the Lord, in defiance to apparent circumstances, conditions and obstacles. Malnourished faith lacks power to pronounce life. Every day of our lives, we must employ our words in building our world. We employ our declarations in executing the greater reality that is found in God's promises for our life. A closed mouth doesn't get fed! As I pen these words, they are not coming from something I just studied, heard or read. My intention is not to usher you into mere understanding, by sharing a small portion of my personal experience.

My sole desire is to awaken you to revelation and provoke you into encountering this same God, whose given you the same power. The God whose word anchored our hearts, preserved our lives and our future. See, all I had was a word from God that multiple times a day I would audibly speak and declare over my husband and to my husband; I would declare it alone in my kitchen and laundry room to the point where I believe my walls are full of the Holy Ghost. Ps. 118:17, *"I will live and not die and declare [testify of] the works of the Lord"*. I would declare Ps. 103:1-6, *"Bless the Lord oh my soul and all that is within me bless his holy name! Bless the Lord oh my soul and forget not all his benefits: who forgives all your iniquities, who heals all your diseases, who redeems your life from the pit of destruction, who crowns you with loving kindness and tender mercies, who satisfies your mouth with good things so that your youth is renewed like the eagle's. The Lord executes righteousness and justice for all those who are oppressed."* That passage is just too good to not insert it all! These became my battle cry. I would remind God that these were His words, His promises and that His reputation was on the line. I would remind Him that He was our only help and our refuge and that if He didn't save us, we would not be saved. I would remind God that He promised to surround us with songs of deliverance. Once Eric became strong enough to sing and play, God literally allowed him to write the most songs he had ever written in his life. They are the songs of deliverance.

Somewhere along the way, as I would speak the Word out loud, I realized that it was no longer in complete panic, in fear, in striving nor in begging. Something was happening to my heart, my husband's as well. The Word was dispelling darkness I didn't even know I had, and revelation flooded my heart. We had begun to shift from simply quoting the word, to decreeing it with faith and power. We went from quoting verses, to legislating in the spirit.

Yes, we were walking through the valley of the shadow of death, but that's just it; we were walking THROUGH. We realized that the singular purpose of through is to get to another place. This changed everything. Now we were aware and firmly convinced that we were on our way TO healing, TO restoration, TO redemption, TO breakthrough, TO our purpose, TO our future. We refused to die in a place called "through," without arriving at our destination; a place called "to." We continued decreeing the Word and discovered that revelation dismantles perceived fears. You will only be afraid of death so long as you believe it to be powerful and final. Realizing that it is simply a shadow, forever changes your posture in prayer. It's not the valley of death, rather it is the valley of the shadow of death. Turn the light on and shadows disappear. The authority that was birthed in us by decreeing the Word was unlike anything we had ever experienced. The nearness of God's presence even in the valley made us value His abiding presence so much more.

Never did we feel forsaken or forgotten by God. And if for any reason we had a weak moment in our flesh (which there have been too many to count), and we allowed the enemy to get the best of us, we didn't stay there long. We got right back to commanding our emotions to align with God's word, our hearts not to fear and our mountains to move. Yes, you read that correctly. We commanded our own hearts and our own emotions to get in line. David did it! *"Why are you cast down [discouraged, discomforted, dejected, depressed] o my soul? And why are you disquieted within me? Hope in God, for I will yet praise him, who is the health of my countenance, and my God,"* (Ps. 43:5). We commanded our minds not to talk us out of our miracle. Some days were more difficult than others, but we refused to give up. It took years to get to the place where we could command fear to leave our hearts and it obeyed. The response time increased the deeper the Word was established in our hearts. Learning to make strategic and legal decrees has changed our lives. We have whatever we say! So we say it until we believe it, and we believe it until we see it manifest. God will not do just what He said, but what we say.

These days you can find my husband busy in ministry, being a prophet to the entertainment industry and living out his purpose. He's impacting lives. He's back to being the funny, passionate, humble servant he was before, only now with a testimony that makes demons tremble and darkness flee. His life is forever a rebuke to the gates of hell. Now when Eric worships, it's with the first hand knowledge of having experienced God in the valley. Now when he speaks it's with the expectation and belief that everything around him must respond to the word of God in his mouth. When he declares, it is according to the testimony of Jesus over his life. Together we now do for others what Jesus, through the power of His word, did for us; we cancel funerals.

We have learned the power of testimony. We got over all forms of timidity and became bold in audibly decreeing the word. This has been and continues to be a major key to our victory. In John 5:30-45, Jesus is defending His ministry by outlining evidence that proves He is from God. This portion of scripture is referred to as the Fourfold Witness. Jesus proclaims that He has no need of validating himself but that He has four witnesses to speak on His behalf: John The Baptist, His Works, The Father and the Scriptures all testified of him. All four witnesses were able to offer corroborating testimony of who Jesus was, what He said and how He lived. When it comes to living a life of decree, there are four dimensions of witness that must corroborate testimony about what comes out of your mouth.

The first witness is Yahweh. In Ex. 3:13-15 this is the Hebrew name by which God himself chose to be remembered throughout all generations. It is translated as "I AM". People often struggle with trying to find the right thing to say to please God. The reality is we please God by having faith. In regards to our declarations, He's not looking for us to be creative or impressive. He will not override your will so you have to give Him permission by aligning with his word, through your decree. He is just looking for us to simply repeat back to Him what He has already said. There's no need to be deep. It is as simple as saying "God you said in your word that those who put their trust in you will never be put to shame. I believe it and I decree it." The only thing that God understands is His own words. That is all He is obligated to. He hastens His word to perform it (Jer. 1:12). God is essentially tied to his word, so your decree must elicit the witness of His word.

The second dimension is you! Your heart and your soul must bear witness to the decree that you have made. Ps. 62:11 says *"God has spoken once and twice I have heard that [all] power belongs to God."* Is the Psalmist making this statement because there was an immediate echo to

God's voice? How is it that God spoke one time but he heard the declaration twice. I believe that because the Word is incorruptible seed, when God spoke it the first time, it landed on good soil in David's heart. That was the first time he heard that all power belonged to God. The second time he heard the declaration was after the word had taken root in his heart, and then eventually came out of his own mouth. Because faith comes by hearing and hearing by the word of God, you are inevitably going to hear the word that is hidden in your heart again. Seed that is planted eventually turns into harvest. I once heard a man of God say "Every word is a seed. Every seed has a harvest, and every harvest has a due date." You must be diligent in constantly sowing the word into your heart, ensuring a cycle of harvest. In so doing, your own heart bears witness to the decrees that you make. Sometimes the greatest obstacle to breaking through is you. Your heart and your mind left idle and without constant focus on the Word, will deceive you. Your emotions are quick to change, but decreeing the promises of God will anchor your heart, making you steadfast and unmovable.

The third dimension is the witness of the actual mountain. Here's a secret you should tell everyone you can;

MOUNTAINS HAVE EARS. *"Truly I tell you, if anyone says to this mountain, 'Go throw yourself into the sea,' and does not doubt in their heart but believes that what they say will happen, it will be done for them."* (Mark 11:23) Why would Jesus admonish us to command a mountain with our words if it doesn't have the ability to hear us? *"And He arose and rebuked the wind and the waves and said, 'Quiet, be still!' Then the wind died down and it was completely calm."* (Mark 4:39) Even your storms have ears. If they obeyed Jesus and He lives inside of you, it should be no different when you speak. Clearly your breakthrough must be voice activated. Your mountains and storms respond to your command because they know the sound of your voice. When you speak and announce with boldness and authority, power is activated and cancer has to go; depression has to move; lack has to move; infirmity has to move; bondage has to break; curses must be broken. Sometimes we wait for a great man or woman of God to command our mountains and our situations to move. We put our faith in another person instead of realizing that our mountains are going to respond to our own voice. It is imperative that you learn to put your mouth on whatever obstacles are blocking you from purpose and joy.

The fourth and final witness to corroborate your testimony is Satan and all the forces of darkness. According to Ephesians 6, the Word of God is the "Sword of the Spirit". When dealing with a demonic attack, your decrees virtually cut down the works of the enemy. The Word enables you to contend by speaking truth to cancel out every lie of Satan. Rom. 16:19-20 declares, *"...Be wise in doing right and to stay innocent of any wrong. The God of peace will soon crush Satan under your feet."* The enemy ought to testify that he was crushed underneath your feet when you decreed the word of God. You cannot afford to be silent when you come under attack. Open your mouth and wield your spiritual sword. Your fight is not against flesh and blood. You are wrestling against principalities, against powers, against the rulers of darkness of this world and against spiritual wickedness in high places. Eph. 6:12 says you must keep your artillery stocked and your sword sharp. When done correctly, your decrees cause severe damage to the camp of the enemy. They are indeed weapons of mass destruction to the kingdom of darkness.

When Jesus encountered the demoniac living in the Gadarenes, the response of the demons to his presence is very insightful. Never had Jesus physically confronted a demon in scripture. But, He had a reputation even in hell. Devils understood quite well that should He open His mouth their reign of terror was over. They understood that His authority far exceeded theirs and that complete obedience was their only appropriate response. So as Jesus is walking by, minding His own business, the demons begin to cry out, *"What have we to do with You, Jesus, You Son of God? Have you come to torment us before the time?"* (Matt. 8:29) Demons are tormented by the sheer presence of Jesus, which you and I carry. How much more when we pronounce the Word! Discovering that I don't have to be tormented by demonic spirits and assignments, and that in actuality I torment them when I manifest Christ by decreeing His word, changed everything. I believe this revelation can also change everything for you.

CHAPTER 6

LET US REASON TOGETHER

DECREE A THING

Typically the discussion of decreeing has been made into a gimmick. Self- helpers have spoon fed an entire generation the concept of naming it and claiming it. We've been instructed to simply visualize what we desired and that as we speak it, we attract it. As incredibly powerful as our tongues are, God also looks at something else when manifesting our declarations, that is our hearts. We have been invited to sit and reason with God, to essentially plead our case before Him. We must provide evidence in this negotiation setting. Does the desire align with the purpose of God? I would do you a grave injustice if I simply told you to name it and claim it and wait for the check by the mail. Do you want to be healed just to be free from affliction? Do you want to be wealthy just to live lavishly? Do you want a great anointing just to be regarded as being special? There must be redemptive purpose for that healing. When God releases great wealth into your life, how will you use it to impact lives? Will your anointing actually destroy burdens over people's lives or just turn you into a Pharisee; a circus attraction to be seen and applauded by men.

There is something God desires in exchange from you to ensure that you can be trusted with heaven's best; He desires your heart. It is an irresponsible and destructive Gospel that obligates God to our bidding, solely based on our declaration. God has a mind, a heart, an agenda, a desire and a purpose that needs a vehicle to be released into the earth realm. When our declaration is no longer just based on us having our way, but facilitating his Kingdom agenda, our prayers and declarations will manifest. We don't ever negotiate with hell, but when we're invited to negotiate at the King's table, we must come prepared with our offering. What are we willing to sow? What price are we willing to pay in exchange for what we want released from His Hand? Job 22:27 which says, *"You will make your prayer to Him. He will hear you, and you will PAY YOUR VOWS."* isn't as quoted, beloved nor as well known as the verse that follows. But it holds a major key to manifesting the promise and power of verse 28 which says *"You shall also decree a thing, and it shall be established for you, and light will shine on your way."*

Please don't tune me out. I know You may be shaking your head wondering "Wait, so I've got to pay something?" I wish I could tell you that you were completely absolved of any responsibility. That all you had to do was just love Jesus and go around with a magical Moses styled staff that just made miracles happen, with the slightest touch. Sorry to be the one to dash that fantasy. A life of fruitful declaration requires that we actually partner with God and invest into our breakthrough. We must participate in our own deliverance and sow into our own miracle. Don't worry, this is not the part where I instruct you to sow a thousand dollar seed offering into my ministry to unlock your overflow, I promise. *The Benson Bible Commentary* gives great insight into how Job 22:27 translates from the Hebrew. "*Thou shall multiply thy prayers.*" Wow! It isn't a basic and habitual prayer that produces manifestation of one's decree. It is the multiplied prayer, dare I say the life of prayer, the life spent in adoration and at the feet of Jesus that generates potency. God expects me to multiply my prayer not for the sake of busy work, but because time spent with Him aligns my desires to those desires of His heart, for me. It is impossible to truly seek God in Spirit and in truth and your heart not become changed. When there is genuine pursuit, He will hear you. You'll find yourself no longer praying what seems or feels good to you. A direct result of gazing into His face is what births a longing to want what He wants, to pray His heart.

The phrase "You will pay your vow" is such strong language in our modern day culture. It wouldn't have been strong for the people living back when this beautiful story of Job's redemption and restoration took place. The millennial believer, whether actually generationally categorized a millennial or not, has difficulty with "paying" anything. Now let me be sure to create some context here. Ridiculous amounts of money are spent for entertainment, great food, and self grooming including clothes, shoes, and cosmetics. People spend thousands of dollars, even go into debt, to attend a 3-day convention based on their favorite movie series, dressed up in costume as a favorite superhero. Some spend hundreds sometimes thousands of dollars to attend championship sports games that last for hours, with no eternal value or benefit. Excess has become acceptable and is even celebrated. We tend to want what we want when we want it, and God help anyone who gets in the way; even God. This generation has grown into being beyond entitled and this deeply erroneous belief has become a lens through which God is seen.

Our culture has deceived us into believing that God exists for man as opposed to man existing for God. So, we give so little in forms of devotion, worship, service, pursuit, obedience, tithes and offerings, and yet expect God to just serve at our beck and call. Rather than looking at Yahweh with eyes of gratitude, awe, wonder and love, we just need Him to dispense His benefits. *Easton's Bible Dictionary* defines a vow as *"a solemn promise deliberately and freely made to God to perform a good work or to abstain from performing a certain thing for a limited period or sometimes for life."* The very first vow in the Bible is made by Jacob, one of the Patriarchs, in Gen. 28:20-22. *"Then Jacob made a vow saying, 'If God will be with me and will watch over me on this journey I am taking and will give me food to eat and clothes to wear so that I return safely to my father's household, then the LORD will be my God. And this stone that I have set up as a pillar will be God's house, and of all that you give me I will give you a tenth.'"* When you read the entire passage and get a sense of what was happening with Jacob at that time, you quickly realize that he needed major intervention from God. He needed something supernatural that only Yahweh could perform. His vow was simple, but came from a pure heart, which God knew was trustworthy. So many people made or took vows in the Bible: Job, Sampson, David, Hannah, and Daniel just to name a few. What is so remarkable about these Biblical figures is that because they honored their vows, God in turn honored them.

God gave Hannah a son, and she kept her vow by bringing him to live at the temple as promised. God honored her and blessed her with 5 more children. Daniel vowed to the Lord to fast and pray, and was honored by being made a high ranking authority in the very same system that tried to kill him. Taking a vow as directed by Holy Spirit, can be a powerful tool in shifting angels and principalities alike. It further draws the attention of heaven to the heart of the man or woman who is resolved to see God move. Making the vow however, is not where we falter, if we remember to make one at all. It is in paying or fulfilling the vow with diligence that we struggle. Some make a vow out of sheer desperation, as though Yahweh can't see our hearts and can be bribed or manipulated. Remember the Apostle Paul's admonishment, *"Do not be deceived, God is not mocked..."* (Gal. 6:7). Others are so inconsistent during the period of their vow and just rely on sloppy grace to "cover them". And then there are those who receive whatever it is they wanted from God, yet they fail to come back to say thank you. It's fair to deduce that statistically speaking one out of ten return after their miracle to pay their vow. That is a frightening thought because this means that only ten percent of people ever really give God the payment they owe Him, whether that is in the form of praise, worship, service, sacrifice or even finances. But for those who may want to argue that vows are an Old Testament concept or ritual, I beg you, please don't harden your heart. God is the same yesterday today and forever. The God of the Old Testament is the same God in the New Testament. Jesus himself declared in John 14:9, "... *Whoever has seen me has seen the Father.*" The Father has not changed.

Jesus also said in Matt. 5:37, "*But let your yes be yes and your no be no. For whatever is more than these is from the evil one.*" He is basically saying that If we make a vow or promise to God, there is no gray area. Our yes needs to be yes. We can't be double minded; we can't be decided one day and then undecided the next. We cannot assume that our breakthrough will come easily and without cost. We can't think that nothing will be required of us and that a simple positive confession will suffice. Without going too deep, I really believe that some have come under unnecessary curses because we have failed to pay on our vows. When Sampson violated his Nazarite vow he lost his strength, he lost his vision and ultimately his life. Now that will preach!!! Our generation places little to no value on a person's word. Most have been so disappointed by people that it is nearly impossible to believe in promises or oaths. This mindset is a major detriment in dealing with God, who always keeps His word. As His children, we are called to keep our promises, our word and our oath, especially when made to God. Failing or neglecting to honor our vows to God literally breaks covenant. In so doing we exclude ourselves from being able to experience God as our strength, our vision and our life. What is a life without vision? And what is vision without the strength to execute? Because the gifts and calling of God are irrevocable, Sampson was still graced to function in his gift within a corporate setting.

God still used him in a powerful way to defeat the Philistines despite his lack of personal vision and victory. It is critical that we not mistake the continual flow and function of our gifts as God exempting us from honoring our covenantal vows. We can be delinquent in our vow to God but still be used by God. Gifts are not for the individual, they operate for the purpose of edifying the people of God. They are never to be used solely to gauge the condition of relationship between God and the administrator of the gift. As you read this book, if you have made a vow that you have not fulfilled, I am pleading with you, repent and course correct.

In Luk.7, we are introduced to a Roman Centurion who is a man of great power, wealth, and authority. He's entrusted with a great deal of responsibility with many men and servants. Now, he serves at the mercy of the Emperor, so he understands that his power and authority are for a greater purpose. When his beloved servant falls ill, we can assume that with all the resources he had available to him, he had done all he could to save his life. Perhaps he had sought the best care and the best doctors but nothing had worked in curing his servant. This is when The Centurion sends word to Jesus, at which, He begins to go heal the servant. This is a crucial moment in the story. Jesus is heading to the Centurion's house to fulfill his request. Up until that point everyone who had come asking for a miracle had the benefit of Jesus' physical presence. The Man at the Pool of Bethesda, Bartimaeus (whom I hate calling "Blind" because that was a temporary condition healed by Jesus. For some reason church culture insists on perpetually labeling that man based on circumstance.) among others, had encountered Jesus in person. But The Centurion, decides to reason with Jesus. He lays out his case, stating that he is unworthy of having Jesus in his home. The greatest argument presented, takes on a different angle.

Based on his experience as a man under great authority, who in turn also operates in delegated authority he understood the power of a command. He describes how his servants come and go at his command and accomplish whatever he requires of them, solely based on his words. This Centurion was able to connect the relationship between himself and his servants and the relationship between Jesus and His words. He understood that words were equivalent to servants. And when spoken with authority they would produce. This was the very first time that Jesus was being sought out to perform a miracle, without him physically being present. But this man of great faith, had discovered that Jesus' breath, His Spirit, His Power, His authority rested on His declaration. His words were servants that had to fulfill and accomplish everything He had sent them forth to do, and they could not return void. The Centurion, with delegated or borrowed authority, generated movement from a hundred men at his command. Jesus had all authority in heaven and on earth. How much more would His words, which were His foot soldiers, swiftly execute his command?

When we reason with heaven, it is inevitable that revelation is ignited. When we go before Jesus, His mere presence unlocks the loins of our understanding. Because He is light, His words bring light. Once asked why so many miracles would take place in his crusades, one of the most beloved and effective Evangelists of our times, Reinhard Bonnke, said "I believe that God's word in His mouth is the same as God's word in my mouth." Wow! What he was saying is that the ability of God's word to produce does not change whether it is in His own mouth or in our mouth. When we are full of the light of God, and have been transformed by being in His presence, the Word that we speak will produce. It will shift atmospheres, it will cancel curses, it will reverse demonic death decrees, it will change the destiny of nations. The Word in our mouth will raise the dead and open blind eyes. It will activate supernatural favor and break the chains of addiction off our loved ones. The Word in our mouth will restore broken relationships and will rebuke forces of darkness. Not only is there power in your declaration when you say what God says but there is a miracle in your mouth. Determine to reason with God, according to His word.

CHAPTER 7

THE LAW OF GRAVITY

DECREE A THING

Gravity! It works whether you believe in it or not. It is a law of the universe established by God, in His infinite wisdom. You can decide that you are going to defy gravity and jump off of the tallest building in your city. It goes without saying that your personal beliefs will have no bearings on your impending funeral! I know that's a little dark, but it's true. A law designed by Yahweh, does not afford us the option of exempting ourselves, solely based on our personal belief. You remember the saying don't you? What goes up must come down.

There are laws set in motion that are automatic. We don't have to understand every mechanical aspect to know it works. Another such law being, sowing and reaping. No matter who you are, where you come from, what you believe, everyone has an internal awareness of reciprocity. Hindu, Buddhist, Christian, Muslim or Atheist, we all get it. We all understand that what you put out, comes back to you. In one way or another, you will reap what you sow, whether it is good or it is bad. Best displayed in nature, this law manifests all around us.

A single seed is planted and after a while, produces more of its own kind. Naturally, watermelon seeds produce more watermelon. Orange seeds will never produce apples. There is an unseen force at work that ensures every seed, once released into good soil, and properly cared for, brings forth harvest after the appropriate amount of time has elapsed. Much of what our lives have resulted in is due to seeds sown by parents, teachers, our communities at large and our choices and decisions along the way. Seeds are the framework that produce the harvest we call our reality.

The Law of Confession: Yes, you have what you say... it is a law! You will even have what you fear. That's critical because what we fear can be so instrumental in dictating what we speak and confess. The key thing to remember about operating in this space is the necessity for surrender to God. Many people believe that the universe is responsible for releasing their blessings or whatever they name and claim. My personal conviction is that the universe was created by the same Master Architect who created me. I place my demand and my faith on the Creator of heaven and earth, whom I believe is Yahweh. That's not to take away anyone's right to believe differently.

In creating you and me, Yahweh deposited His very own image and likeness into us. This means that like our Creator, we have been endowed with a creative force released through our breath. Our breath by the way is borrowed. God lends us His breath and His life and His Spirit for however long we walk this earth. So in speaking, we simply attach sound to spirit and engage the resident power to create, like our Father. I love John 6:63, *"it is the Spirit that gives life. The flesh profits nothing. The words that I have spoken to you are Spirit and they are life."* Jesus reveals two highly significant truths in this verse.

The first truth is that it's not enough to have something in your possession, you've got to speak to it. If you have a marriage, a family, a business, a career, an ability, a vision, an aspiration, you must speak to it. Your words will establish the identity of what you possess and set the trajectory of its future. So just as we belong to Jesus, and are His prized possession, He speaks and declares words of life into our lives. He is not content with just having us. He speaks life, purpose, and destiny to us. The second thing Jesus reveals is a clear definition of why our words are so powerful. Remember we are made in His similitude or likeness, meaning we have His ability. He equates His words to Spirit and Life. As defined by *Easton's Bible Dictionary* "*ruach*" is the Hebrew word for spirit. It also means wind or breath. When you open your mouth, attaching words to sound (wind), you are releasing Spirit and Life. You are prophesying and giving direction to what is authorized to exist in that marriage, that family, that body, that career, that vision, etc... So not only is it critical that you speak and declare but WHAT you speak is of the utmost importance.

Coming into relationship with Yahweh creates a safety rail, for your heart, called His will. See, His perfect will not only secures my desires, but ensures I receive what I'm decreeing at the right time. Why is that important? Because the right thing at the wrong time will destroy you. So many people tap into all types of otherworldly forces to gain access to the fruit of their confession. Many times they are crushed under the weight of that supposed "blessing" because they weren't ready. There wasn't enough of a space created in their life to handle what they prayed for. It may not even be a blessing assigned to their life. Other times, the blessing becomes a burden, gets neglected or squandered because maturity and pure intentions are absent. And worse of all, the presumed blessing may come from a source other than God, and that dear friends is a nightmare.

Think about a person you know who made declarations and decrees about a mate. They met someone, fell madly in love and just knew that this was from God. They knew that this was the manifestation they'd believed for. So, when things go south a few months or a couple of years into it and this person is literally a monster, was it still from God? Your same friend will tell you that this person is the devil himself. How did they go from being a blessing to being Satan? You guessed it, maybe they weren't from God to begin with. The person simply provided your friend with an opportunity to realize what they had wanted, so bold red flags were ignored.

I don't just want to decree something and then receive it, only to be destroyed by it. See, the blessing of the Lord makes rich and adds no sorrow. (Prov. 10:22) When your harvest comes from Yahweh, there's no drama or trauma. It's in the timing of God, and will be received and celebrated. Job 22:28 *"and you will also decree a thing and it shall be established for you; So light will shine on your ways."* When your decree is centered in the perfect will of God, and it produces manifestation at the right time there will be light. The end result of a Godly decree is that there is clarity and light. God himself will shine His light on you, when what you have decreed, according to His word, is established in your life. A true blessing does not require manipulation, compromise, lying, cheating or stealing. The light that results from it, serves as evidence that God's hand is on it.

The Word works because God honors His own word and has placed it above all His names, according to Ps. 138:2. We are never to use the word to speak destruction or death on people. We are not to manipulate the word to satisfy selfish desires and think that there is no consequence. If you destroy a marriage and take someone else's wife or husband because you believe God has answered your declaration and prayer, please beware. You will reap what you have sown and will incur consequences on your bloodline that your children and grandchildren may have to endure. This is unless they break the curse off of their lives and disconnect themselves from the yolk of that sin. Decreeing and declaring is never to be weaponized against people.

Now if someone is legitimately hurting you and is trying to destroy you, you can pray against the demonic spirits in operation in the person to be broken by the love and power of God. You can ask God to fill that individual's heart with His love and you can decree that they grant you favor and grace. I've personally experienced this years ago, by a former manager, who persecuted me. It didn't matter what I did or how pure my heart was, or how good my intentions were, it was never good enough. I would come home and cry to my husband about how I just wanted to say something in return and speak my mind, but Holy Spirit would not let me. Instead, He gave me a strategy.

He had me begin decreeing blessings, favor, and promotion over that manager everyday. He instructed me to begin praying for this individual and their family. Even though, this person had blocked me from getting well earned raises, promotions and would purposefully minimize any great achievement I accomplished. To say this was difficult or challenging is a huge understatement. It took time for my heart to mean those prayers and make those declarations in all sincerity. Let me rephrase that, it took a long time. Nearly a year to be exact. But I literally came to work one morning and learned that a sudden decision had been made to move this person to a different area. Upper management may have had a great reason for making this move, but as far as I was concerned, I had decreed my way right out from being under an oppressive leader. And in similar "suddenly" fashion, I myself was given a significant promotion seemingly overnight. I didn't even apply for it. God simply allowed me to reap what I had sown as I declared promotion and blessing for somebody else.

It is my hope and prayer that, thus far, this book has brought some enlightenment, encouragement, and awareness to the power you have been so generously given by Abba. I hope that, perhaps, it has brought a forgotten truth back to your remembrance. Maybe it has yielded an aha moment that will help you embark on your personal journey of decreeing God's word over your life. It's a journey I myself plan on never ending. Hopefully, I have shared some keys to help you release the good treasure that is in abundance in your heart. I pray that you have been provoked to open your mouth and decree life over everything around you. There is so much more than can be said, and that has been said on the subject matter of decreeing. I honestly didn't just want to put more information out there, for the sake of releasing information. While this book is certainly not exhaustive, I do firmly believe that if you'll prayerfully put these principles into practice, your life will never be the same. They have certainly changed my life forever. I'm not different from you nor, am I better than you. I just sincerely want to live out what I say I believe. I want to see the God that I worship, pray to and sing about, moving in my life. I want to see the signs, wonders and miracles that I read about in the book of Acts, manifesting in my life, as I decree the word of God.

The following section is meant to inspire you and aid you as you start decreeing a new reality for yourself. Honestly I wish I had had something like this, a compilation of thematic declarations that I could reference in my prayer times. I had to search out the scriptures, as I was led by Holy Spirit, and began writing these decrees in my journal. I would place post it notes filled with scriptures on my mirrors around the house. They were on our refrigerator, on the banister leading upstairs, basically anywhere I knew my eyes would rest long enough to be reminded of what God had promised me and my family. So for those of you reading this who are serious, I have some homework for you. I bet you weren't expecting that! You are going to incorporate one of these decrees into your prayer time daily. It is completely up to you if you want to use a different one everyday. But I would recommend using the same one over the course of a week. This will allow the word to get rooted in your heart as you pray and decree it. You might even find that you feel led to go for two weeks on a single one. But ultimately just don't be in a rush. The idea is not to check this off of your to do list, but to allow the Word to shift your thinking, your beliefs and therefore your confessions.

So here is what you will need to do:

- Worship: if you are like me, it gets a little loud in your head, so worship is an amazing way to quiet your mind and focus your heart on beholding Jesus. He's so beautiful!

- Adoration: This is when you use your own words to magnify God. Out loud, recite the wonderful things that He has done. Remember you have to enter into His courts with praise.

- Decree: Take one of the decrees and speak it out loud. You don't have to scream but speak it loud enough to where you hear it. Remember that faith comes by hearing and hearing by the word of God. Insert your name in it wherever possible. Decree it over your children, husband, or wife. Be prepared with your journal to write down specific strategies and instructions Holy Spirit speaks as you do this.

- Consider making a vow to take this journey for 21 days. Yes, commit before God to engage in decreeing his word over your life everyday for 3 weeks. Some of you may even feel led to do it twice daily during those three weeks, and may even decide to include some form of fasting. Set a calendar or alarm on your phone to remind you. Add it to your family's daily list of activities if you choose to do it together. Holy Spirit may even instruct you to sow a special financial seed to your local church, separate from your normal giving. Just do it! I believe that God will completely overhaul your heart during your vow. Your miraculous life change won't be far behind. I'm believing with you.

- START NOW. Don't put it off for a more opportune time. Satan will always find ways to keep you from engaging in the Word. There is no time like the present so go ahead and get started.

- Write out your own legal decree that you will sign and date, at the very end of this book. My ultimate goal is to have equipped you with a template that you can turn around and use to create your own decree. One thing's for sure, you can be as specific with yours as needed. It's between you and God.

CHAPTER 8

DECREES

DECREE A THING

GATES:

I declare and I decree that I'm entering His gates with thanksgiving. Because of this my gates will always be open, they will never be shut, Day or night. People are bringing me the wealth of nations. (Isa. 60:11) People I don't know, people from near and far are compelled to pour wealth into my life. There's a constant flow of increase coming through my gates. There is no stagnation, there is no delay, there is no interruption at my gate. I decree that there is justice at my gate. People who don't like me find themselves desperately needing to favor and bless me. Even the hidden and secret treasures of nations are coming to me. Nations, systems, industries and mountains of culture are unlocked to me.

I decree that I, as a gate, I lift up my head and that the King of Glory is coming in. (Ps. 24:9) I am in position for manifestation. The glory of the King, which is His reputation, His influence, His splendor, His weight, His fame, His wealth, and His power are resting on me. The Lord, strong and mighty in battle, enters in. My head is lifted high above my enemies, fearlessly and shamelessly. I am the gate of heaven and angels are ascending and descending in my life. I live under an open heaven in Jesus name (Gen. 28:17-18).

SPIRITUAL GROWTH:

I decree in the name of Jesus and by the authority God has given me as His signet ring (Hag. 2:23), I am a lover of God's presence. I was created to love Him with all my heart, mind, body and soul (Matt. 22:37). I decree that my thirst and my appetite for God is increasing. I will pursue His presence and seek His face (Ps. 42:1; Ps. 27:4). I press into worship, I devour the word, I am changed by the word (Eph. 5:26) because I am a doer of the word. I study to show myself approved, rightly dividing the word of truth (2 Tim. 2:15). I decree that I am disciplined in meditating on the word. I pray without ceasing. I am quick to hear the voice of Holy Spirit and even quicker to obey. I come to God because I believe that He alone is my God. I decree that He rewards me with the bread of His presence as I diligently seek Him (Heb. 11:6) His face is my reward. His voice is my reward.

I decree that I am growing into the full stature of Christ. I decree that the eyes of my understanding are open to know the hope of His calling (Eph. 1:18). I am a fruitful tree and I bear much fruit that remains (John 15:15-17). I am a fruitful vine near a spring, whose branches climb over a wall (Gen. 49:22). I am the planting of the Lord

(Isa. 61:3) and I flourish in the House of God (Ps. 92:13). I decree that I am steadfast and unmovable. I have been sealed by Holy Spirit as a guarantee of God's promise concerning me (Eph. 1:13; 2 Cor. 1:22). The fruit of the Spirit is in abundance in my life. I walk in love, joy, peace, forbearance, kindness, goodness, faithfulness, gentleness and self control (Gal. 5:22-23). I decree that I daily surrender, yielding to the work of Holy Spirit in my life. I am the aroma of Christ to God, among those who are being saved and those who are perishing (2 Cor. 2:15). My life is a testament to the love, the goodness, the mercy and the grace of God.

THE MIND OF CHRIST:

I decree in the name of Jesus and by the authority God has given me as His signet ring, that I have the mind of Christ (1 Cor. 2:16). My thoughts are renewed daily (Rom. 12:2). I am not enslaved to fear for I have been given the spirit of power, love and a sound mind (2 Tim. 1:7). I decree that I starve fear and feed faith daily. I think on the things that are above, not below. I think on what is pure, lovely, holy and of a good report (Phil. 4:8) I decree that I am not anxious, I am not nervous, nor am I depressed. I do not meditate on the wrong information, but rather I focus on the finished work of the cross. I decree that guilt and shame can not paralyze me (Rom. 10:11). All manner of tormenting thoughts are uprooted from my imagination.

I decree that my mind is not the devil's playground. It is never idle. My mind is renewed and transformed by the word of God. I cast down imaginations and demolish arguments (2 Cor. 10:5) My mind is the birthing place of God ideas, witty inventions, problem solving solutions, innovation, creativity, and business ideas (Prov. 8:12; Deut. 8:18). My mind is not in a daze. I operate with clarity and understanding. I am never confused or forgetful, for the memory of the righteous is blessed (Prov. 10:7).

I am alert. I am able to meditate on God's word and his goodness, without distraction or loss of focus. I decree that I am not plagued by anxiety, stress or depression. I am in perfect peace with my mind focused on Jesus (Isa. 26:3; Phil. 4:7). The same mind which was in Christ Jesus is also in me. The spirit of wisdom, knowledge and understanding rests heavily upon my life. I decree that as a man thinks in his heart so is he (Prov. 23:7). I align my thoughts with what God thinks about me. I am a well watered garden. I am a joint heir with Christ Jesus. I am an interruption to curses in my blood line. I am crowned with praise and fame. I am God's masterpiece. God delights in prospering me. I am chosen. I am accepted. I am forgiven. I am loved.

VICTORY IN SPIRITUAL WARFARE:

I decree in the name of Jesus and by the authority God has given me as His signet ring that I am victorious in spiritual warfare. I put on the full armor of God. My loins are girded with truth. My heart is hidden by the breastplate of righteousness. My feet are blessed with the preparation of the gospel of peace. I am an instrument of peace. I actively take up the shield of faith to extinguish every fiery dart of the enemy (Eph. 6:10-18). I put on the helmet of salvation, the gift I have received by grace, through faith. I take up the sword of the Spirit, which is the Word of God, to cut down and dismantle every lie of the evil one. I am covered by the precious and powerful blood of Jesus (Heb. 9:12-14) I dwell In the secret place of The Most High and the battle is not mine but belongs to the Lord. (1 Sam. 17:47) He teaches my hands to make war and my fingers to make battle (Ps. 144:1). I decree that I have divine insight and strategy given by Holy Spirit. I recognize the devices of the enemy (2 Cor. 2:11). I draw a bloodline and blood-block every manner of demonic attack. I decree that as I am excellent at what is good and I am innocent of evil, the God of peace is crushing Satan underneath my feet. (Rom. 16:19-20)

I reverse every curse, cancel every indictment, and silence every accusation (Gal. 3:13; Rev. 12:10). I decree that every unrighteous vow is broken, soul ties severed, demonic cycles destroyed. I have been given authority to recalibrate my spiritual environment. God's word in my mouth is the same as God's word in His own mouth (Rom. 10:8). I decree that Jehovah Gibbor opposes those who oppose me. The Lion of Judah fights my battles, and is great in me. My God causes me to triumph and overcome every time. (2 Cor. 2:14) My God is shaking the heavens and the earth. He is overthrowing royal thrones and destroying the power foreign kingdoms. He is overturning their chariots and riders. The horses will fall and their riders will kill each other. (Hag. 2:21-22) I decree that my God has conquered and He has defeated every foe, giving me the victory. I do not labor for victory nor do I fight for it, but rather I enforce it in Jesus name.

FINANCES:

I decree in the name of Jesus and by the authority God has given me as His signet ring that I live in a poverty-free zone. My life is recession proof because I am planted by rivers of living water and I bear fruit in every season (Ps. 1). My God has increased me not just 30, 60 or 100 fold, but 1000 fold (Deut. 1:11). My storage barn is filled with plenty of grain and my vats overflow, bursting with new wine (Prov. 3:10). I am satisfied. The Most High is my shepherd, I have no lack, I want for nothing (Ps. 23:1). Because I honor God with the first fruit of all my increase, He rebukes the devourer from me. I am willing and obedient, therefore I eat the good of the land. I have more than enough (Isa. 1:19). My bills are paid on time because God withholds no good thing from me. Abundance and increase consistently flow to me, as I walk uprightly. God has bestowed me with favor and honor (Ps. 84:11). My God supplies all my needs according to His riches in glory, in Christ Jesus. I live in the glory. Supernatural resources are available to me in the glory (Phil. 4:19)

I am a good steward. I give freely and it is returned to me good measure, pressed down and shaken together. People, even strangers, will pour into my lap (Luk. 6:38).

I am a lender and am never held captive as a borrower (Prov. 22:7). I owe nothing to anyone but love (Rom. 13:8). The poverty mindset is broken off of me and my bloodline. Greed and the need for instant gratification shall never have a hold on my life. I do not hoard money but I manage it with wisdom and integrity. I am not controlled by the love of money, but I trust in God. He will never fail me (Heb.13:5). I will pursue God's presence, His glory and His wisdom more than silver or gold. I don't just survive financially, I thrive, I excel and I build wealth. I am the good man who leaves an inheritance to my grandchildren (Prov. 13:22). I underwrite their future. I secure my children's financial legacy. The blessing of the Lord on my life makes me rich and He adds no sorrow with it (Prov. 10:22). I am a distributor, a steward, a treasurer with full access to the treasury. I am trustworthy with God's money. I am wise and I am generous. Overflow is my permanent reality.

HEALING:

I decree in the name of Jesus and by the authority God has given me as His signet ring that I was healed. Before sickness showed up, healing was already provided, by the stripes of Jesus (1 Pet. 2:24). I diligently listen to the voice of the Lord, give ear to His commandments and I keep all His statutes. None of the diseases of the Egyptians will come upon me because He is the Lord my healer (Ex. 15:26). God's blessing is on my food and water. He's taken sickness away from me (Ex. 23:25). I decree that divine healing is my portion and inheritance. God sent His word and healed all my diseases. He delivered me from destruction (Ps.107:20). I am healed physically. No infections, harmful bacteria, parasites, airborne diseases, terminal conditions, diseases of the blood, or hereditary curses can survive in my body. Because I am the righteousness of God in Christ, Even my bones are protected by the Lord. Not one of them is broken (Ps. 34:20). I decree that my organs function at optimal capacity. Every system in my body responds to the word of God and comes into proper alignment.

I declare that I am healed emotionally. Because God heals the brokenhearted and binds up their wounds, I am restored (Ps. 147:3) I am healed from all trauma, abuse, sorrow, neglect, rejection, false accusations and disappointment. My heart is joyful, therefore a crushed spirit will not dry up my bones (Prov. 17:22). My light breaks forth like the dawn and my healing comes quickly (Isa. 58:8). Because dunamis power is released to me now, I decree that I am excellent of soul. Premature death is not my portion. I decree that death by accident, death by sickness, by heart attack, by murder, nor self inflicted death will not operate in my life. God will satisfy me with long life and show me His salvation (Ps. 91:16). I will not die but live and declare the works of the Lord (Ps. 188:17). The son of righteousness rises upon me with healing in his wings and his beams (Mal. 4:2). His presence burns up every evil work of sickness and infirmity in my life. I am healed. I am whole.

WISDOM:

I decree in the name of Jesus and by the authority God has given me as His signet ring that wisdom is my portion. I decree that I love wisdom, I pursue wisdom, I operate in wisdom. I am the righteous child of God, whose mouth utters wisdom and my tongue speaks what is just (Ps. 37:30). As I please God, He gives me wisdom so I can effectively apply what I know (Eccl. 2:26). In all my getting I obtain understanding. I know what to do, when to do it and how to do it (Prov. 4:7). The riches of complete understanding are unfolded to me, as I seek Christ in whom are hidden all the treasures of wisdom and knowledge (Col. 2:2-3). I decree that God can trust me with His secrets, His thoughts, and His plans. I trust God to generously give me wisdom for any area where I lack it (Jam.1:5). I decree that wisdom manifests in my understanding, in revelation, prophetic insight and even in my dreams.

I decree that I am wise in managing my relationships. In wisdom I discern with whom I can share my heart. I make wise decisions concerning my family, my spouse, and my children. I apply wisdom to my finances, my career and my health. As I find wisdom and I gain understanding, I am blessed (Prov. 3:13). I am blessed beyond measure. I am counted among the wise, even as I embrace discipline (Prov. 19:20). By wisdom I enter into the fullness of the promise of God for my life. By wisdom I breakthrough every demonic assignment of delay and I am accelerated in purpose. I decree that wisdom is the foundation of my walled city. I will not perish for the lack of knowledge (Hos. 4:6). I decree that I will never turn my back on God's wisdom. Because of this, I am kept safe. I am protected from ruin and destruction (Prov. 4:6).

AWAKENING:

I decree in the name of Jesus and by the authority God has given me as His signet ring that I am awake. I arise from spiritual slumber and awaken to the movement of God in my life. I decree that as I awake, Christ is giving me light (Eph. 5:14). Spirits of slumber that have attached themselves to my life are broken now. They are evicted from my spiritual capacity, from my pursuit of God's presence. Slumber is evicted from my ability to walk in my purpose. I will not miss my visitation (Luk. 19:44). I arise from the ashes, I come up from what was meant to immobilize me. I decree that it is my time to arise and shine for my light has come. The glory of the Lord is risen on me (Isa. 60:1) I awaken to the glory of God that is on my life. I receive it, I embrace it, I can see it.

I arise from slumber induced by sorrow (Luk. 22:45). I cast off heaviness, woundedness, offense, mourning and depression. Fear and trauma will no longer paralyze me. I break the spirit of poverty that is rooted in slumber. I decree that as I stay awake I have provision to spare (Prov. 20:13). There is an awakening in my body. I call my entire being to awaken. Spirit of Might, awaken within me. Spirit of Counsel come. Vision come forth and revelation arise in me. I decree that my eyes are wide awake to see the goodness of the Lord in the land of the living.

CONGRATULATIONS

You are now ready to establish your very own decree. Remember that a decree is a legal declaration that God will honor, as you honor Him. Be sure to be led by the Spirit of God as you begin.

There are no rules. Your decree can be based around a specific theme such as love, or faith. It can also be a wholistic approach as to what you are legislating in the spirit for your life, your family, your health or even your finances. You can compose and sign alone or invite your spouse or children to participate.

The following pages are blank for you to write out your legal documents in any format you select. Just be sure to sign at the end. Thank you for taking this journey with me.

Decree Focus/Theme_____

_____

Scriptures that speak to this theme:

1._____

2._____

3._____

4._____

I decree in the name of Jesus and by the authority God has given me as His signet ring that

Decreed by _____

Date_____

Decree Focus/Theme_____

_____

Scriptures that speak to this theme:

1._____

2._____

3._____

4._____

I decree in the name of Jesus and by the authority God has given me as His signet ring that

Decreed by _____

Date_____

Decree Focus/Theme_____

_____

Scriptures that speak to this theme:

1._____

2._____

3._____

4._____

I decree in the name of Jesus and by the authority God has given me as His signet ring that

Decreed by _____

Date_____

Decree Focus/Theme_____

_____

Scriptures that speak to this theme:

1._____

2._____

3._____

4._____

I decree in the name of Jesus and by the authority God has given me as His signet ring that

Decreed by _____

Date_____

Decree Focus/Theme_____

_____

Scriptures that speak to this theme:

1._____

2._____

3._____

4._____

I decree in the name of Jesus and by the authority God has given me as His signet ring that

Decreed by _____

Date_____

Decree Focus/Theme_____

_____

Scriptures that speak to this theme:

1._____

2._____

3._____

4._____

I decree in the name of Jesus and by the authority God has given me as His signet ring that

DECREE A THING

Decreed by _____

Date_____

Decree Focus/Theme_____

_____

Scriptures that speak to this theme:

1._____

2._____

3._____

4._____

I decree in the name of Jesus and by the authority God has given me as His signet ring that

Decreed by _____

Date_____

Decree Focus/Theme_____

_____

Scriptures that speak to this theme:

1._____

2._____

3._____

4._____

I decree in the name of Jesus and by the authority God has given me as His signet ring that

Decreed by _____

Date_____

NOTES

Scriptures	Page
John 1 NKJV	p.2
Gen 1:26-28 NKJV	p.6
Gen 2:7 NKJV	p.7
Ps 118, 119:30 NKJV	p.10
Ps 27:3, Job 13:15, Matt 3:17 KJV	p.12
Rom 8:14 KJV	p.13
Ps 139:16 NKJV	p.15
Ps 119:105 KJV *(paraphrase)*	p.18
Gen 1:2 NKJV	p.26
Job 22:28 NKJV	p.27
Rom 10:8 NIV, Prov 10:11 KJV	p.29
Luk 6:45 NKJV	p.30
Ps 100:4 KJV	p.32
1 Pet 5:8 ESV	p.33
Rom 10:10 KJV	p.34
Oba 1:17 KJV *(paraphrase)*	p.36
Ps 139:17-18 NLT	p.42
Isa 1:19 ESV	p.43
1 Pet 5:6 NKJV	p.44
Rev 12:11 NKJV	p.46
Rom 8:16 NKJV *(reference)*	p.53
Matt 6:11 KJV	p.58
Ps 118:17 NKJV *(paraphrase)*	p.59
Ps 103:1-6 NKJV	p.59
Ps 43:5 KJV *(paraphrase)*	p.62
John 5:30-45 NKJV	p.63
Ex 3:13-15 NKJV, Jer 1:12 KJV, Ps 62:11 NKJV	p.64
Mark 11:23, Mark 4:39 NIV	p.66
Eph 6:17, 6:12 NKJV *(reference)*	p.67

Rom 16:19-20 NLT	p.67
Matt 8:29 NKJV	p.68
Job 22:27-28 NKJV	p.71
Gen 28:20-22 NIV	p.74
Gal 6:7 NKJV	p.75
John 14:9 ESV, Matt 5:37 NKJV	p.76
Luk 7 NKJV	p.78
John 6:63 NKJV	p.84
Prov 10:22 *(reference)*, Job 22:28 NKJV	p.86
Ps 138:2 NKJV	p.87
Decree Scriptures	**Page**
Isa 60:11, Ps 24:9, Gen 28:17-18	p.96
Hag 2:23, Matt 22:37, Ps 42:1, Ps 27:4, Eph 5:26, 2 Tim 2:15, Heb 11:6, Eph 1:18, John 15:15-17, Gen 49:22	p.97
Isa 61:3, Ps 92:13, Eph 1:13, 2 Cor 1:22, Gal 5:22-23, 2 Cor 2:15	p.98
1 Cor 2:16, Rom 12:2, 2 Tim 1:7, Phil 4:8, Rom 10:11, 2 Cor 10:5, Prov 8:12, Deut 8:18, Prov 10:7	p.99
Isa 26:3, Phil 4:7, Prov 23:7	p.100
Eph 6:10-18, Heb 9:12-14, 1 Sam 17:47, Ps 144:1, 2 Cor 2:11, Rom 16:19-20	p.101
Gal 3:13, Rev 12:10, Rom 10:8, 2 Cor 2:14, Hag 2:21-22	p.102
Ps 1, Deut 1:11, Prov 3:10, Ps 23:1, Isa 1:19, Ps 84:11, Phil 4:19, Luk 6:38	p.103
Prov 22:7, Rom 13:8, Heb 13:5, Prov 13:22, Prov 10:22	p.104
1 Pet 2:24, Ex 15:26, Ex 23:25, Ps 107:20, Ps 34:20	p.105
Ps 147:3, Prov 17:22, Isa 58:8, Ps 91:16, Ps 188:17, Mal 4:2	p.106
Ps 37:30, Eccl 2:26, Prov 4:7, Col 2:2-3, Jam 1:5, Prov 3:13	p.107
Prov 19:20, Hos 4:6, Prov 4:6	p.108
Eph 5:14, Luk 19:44, Isa 60:1, Luk 22:45, Prov 20:13	p.109

Works Cited	Page
"Humans need light and interaction to stay sane. Without light, we lose our sense of time, and without interaction, we become consumed with loneliness and boredom. With this sensory deprivation comes the strangest, most unimaginable psychological effects.": Kelly Tatera, "Isolation in the Dark Drives Humans to Brink of Insanity, Studies Find," The Science Explorer, November 19, 2015, http://thescienceexplorer.com/brain-and-body/isolation-dark-drives-humans-brink-insanity-studies-find.	p.20
"thou shall multiply thy prayers": Rev. Joseph Benson, The Benson Bible Commentary (New York: T. Carlton & J. Porter, 1857) https://biblehub.com/commentaries/benson/	p.72
"a solemn promise deliberately and freely made to God to perform a good work or to abstain from performing a certain thing for a limited period or sometimes for life.": M.G. Easton, Easton's Bible Dictionary (New York: Scriptura Press, 2015)	p.74
"God's word in His mouth is the same as God's word in my mouth": Reinhard Bonnke	p.80
"ruach": M.G. Easton, Easton's Bible Dictionary (New York: Scriptura Press, 2015)	p.84

NANCY JOY

Nancy Joy Dozier is a woman on a mission. A devoted wife, mother, entrepreneur, speaker and so much more. A proud native of The Democratic Republic of Congo in Central Africa, she was raised in Boston Massachusetts, in a God fearing home. From a tender age, Nancy had a fervent love for God and was leading adult congregations in worship by the age of ten. Nancy met her husband Eric while they both attended Berklee College of Music in Boston.

Nancy lives on purpose to elevate others into their destinies. As Founder and CEO of Joy Life Enterprises, Nancy serves as a Life Skills Specialist and Personal Pastor. She helps her clients to access their redeemed reality by discovering their divine purpose, resulting in vibrant spiritual lives, increased productivity, and restored vision. In 2017 she launched the "I Am A Miracle" movement, an annual gathering of champions and overcomers. She is dedicated to affecting positive change, especially in the lives of women. With nearly 15 years as a coach Nancy, also an ordained Pastor, considers herself as a cheerleader. Committed to helping women birth their God given dreams, she embraces the role of a spiritual midwife.

Her desire is to inspire all people to become the best versions of themselves, personally, professionally and emotionally. Through various forms of media, speaking engagements, one on one coaching, upcoming books and lifestyle brand, Nancy is giving countless people tools to be strong and to be whole by choosing to live in joy.

CONNECT

—✦—

SOCIALLY WITH NANCY JOY DOZIER:

https://Facebook.com/NancyJoyDozier

Instagram: @NancyJoyDozier

—✦—

YOU CAN LEARN MORE ABOUT NANCY, HER MINISTRY

AND COACHING BY CONNECTING WITH HER AT:
WWW.NANCYJOYDOZIER.COM

FOR BOOKING OR MORE INFO:

contact@nancyjoydozier.com